PLAYTALES

LITTLE RED RIDING HOOD

MOIRA BUTTERFIELD

Heinemann Interactive Library
Des Plaines, Illinois

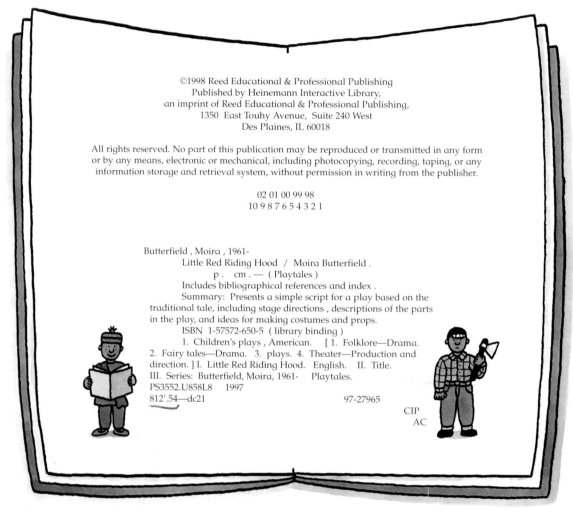

©1998 Reed Educational & Professional Publishing
Published by Heinemann Interactive Library,
an imprint of Reed Educational & Professional Publishing,
1350 East Touhy Avenue, Suite 240 West
Des Plaines, IL 60018

02 01 00 99 98
10 9 8 7 6 5 4 3 2 1

Butterfield , Moira , 1961-
    Little Red Riding Hood / Moira Butterfield .
        p .   cm . — (Playtales)
    Includes bibliographical references and index .
    Summary: Presents a simple script for a play based on the traditional tale, including stage directions , descriptions of the parts in the play, and ideas for making costumes and props.
    ISBN 1-57572-650-5 (library binding)
    1. Children's plays , American.   [1. Folklore—Drama.
2. Fairy tales—Drama. 3. plays. 4. Theater—Production and direction.] I. Little Red Riding Hood. English. II. Title.
III. Series: Butterfield, Moira, 1961-   Playtales.
PS3552.U858L8   1997
812'.54—dc21   97-27965
                                                              CIP
                                                              AC

Co-author: Robin Edwards • Editor: David Riley • Art Director: Cathy Tincknell •
Designer: Anne Sharples • Photography: Trever Clifford • Illustrator: Frances Cony
Props: Anne Sharples

Thanks to: Carlie Townsend, Amy Livesey, George Suttie and Shaka Omwony

Printed and bound in Italy

You will need to use scissors and glue to make the props for your play. Always make sure an adult is there to help you.

Use only water-based face paints and makeup. Children with sensitive skin should use makeup and face paints with caution.

Contents

THE STORY OF LITTLE RED RIDING HOOD

When Red Riding Hood walks through the forest to her Grandma's house, she meets a wicked Wolf who is up to no good. Don't worry, though. Like all good fairy tales, there is a happy ending.

Choose a Part

This play is a story that you can read with your friends and perhaps even act out in front of an audience. You'll need up to five people. Before you start, choose which parts you would like to play.

These two parts can be played by one person.

Red Riding Hood
A kind little girl.

Woodcutter
He appears at the end to save everyone.

Mother
Red Riding Hood's mother appears at the beginning.

Wicked Wolf
A greedy mean wolf who likes to eat people.

Grandma
A sweet old lady who could be a wolf!

Storyteller
Someone who helps tell the tale.

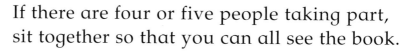

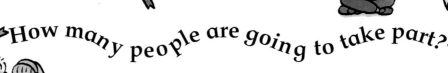

How many people are going to take part?

If there are four or five people taking part, sit together so that you can all see the book.

If there are two or three people, divide the parts between you.

If you want to read the play on your own, use a different sounding voice for each part.

Reading the Play

**Red Riding
Hood**

Wolf

Grandma

Mother

Woodcutter

Storyteller

The play is made up of different lines. Next to each line
there is a name and a picture. This shows who should
be talking.

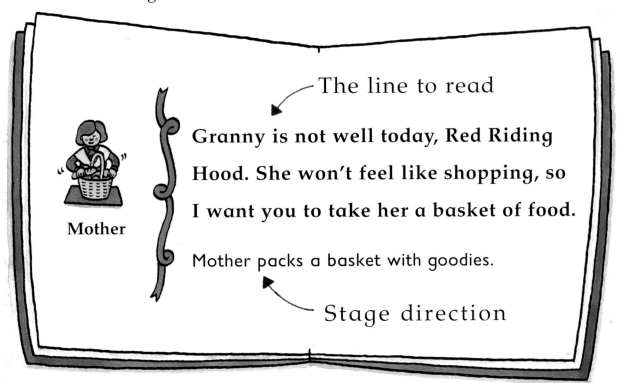

The line to read

**Granny is not well today, Red Riding
Hood. She won't feel like shopping, so
I want you to take her a basket of food.**

Mother packs a basket with goodies.

Stage direction

Mother

In between the lines, there are some stage directions.
They are suggestions for things you might do, such
as, making a noise or acting something out.

Things to Make

Here are some suggestions
for costumes.

RED RIDING HOOD: CLOTHES AND PROPS

Wear a dress and carry a basket of food (borrow some bits and pieces from the kitchen). If you haven't got a basket, a grocery bag will do.

Make a Cloak

You need:
- A piece of red fabric 1yd. square or more
- A strip of fabric 3 in. x 30 in.
- Scissors, pencil, ruler
- A strip of ribbon about 40 in. long
- A needle and thread, or glue

1. Lay the fabric out. Glue or sew a hem along the top and bottom edges.

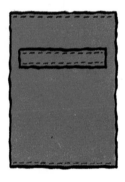

2. Sew or glue the strip of fabric 12 in. from the top edge to make a "channel". Thread the ribbon through.

3. Wrap the cloak around your shoulders and tie the ribbon. Pull the large collar over your head to make a hood.

If you don't want to make a cloak, just wear a red scarf or a red coat with a hood.

Face Painting Ideas

Paint some rosy red cheeks, and freckles around your nose.

WOLF: CLOTHES AND PROPS

Wear a gray T-shirt with a belt tied round your waist and gray leggings or pants.

Make a Tail
You need:
- Scissors
- Three strips of gray fabric or pieces cut from a gray trash bag, 20 in. x 4 in.

1. Snip the bottom edge of each strip to make a fringe. Knot the strips together above the fringes.

2. Braid the strips together.

3. Then knot them together near the top. Now tuck your tail into the back of your belt.

Make a Wolf Mask
You need:
- Some scrap paper and a piece of thin cardboard 8 in. x 10 in.
- Scissors and pencil
- Piece of elastic and glue

Make a mask out of scrap paper first to make sure it fits you. Then copy the size onto the cardboard.

1. Cut the shape of the wolf head and ears out of the cardboard.

2. Cut the eye-holes out of the mask and decorate it. Stick the ears on and thread the elastic at each side to go around the back of your head.

Grandma Disguise
Slip an old nightgown on to become Grandma.

Make a pair of glasses from five pipe cleaners.

Fold an old scarf into a triangle and cut two slits to fit your wolf ears through.

If you are playing both Grandma and the Wolf, don't paint your face because you will need to appear as both characters.

Face Painting Ideas
Paint the end of your nose black and add a black line between your nose and mouth. Put small black dots on your "muzzle".

MOTHER: CLOTHES AND PROPS

Wear a dress and a scarf around your neck. Add a necklace to make you look more grown-up.

WOODCUTTER: CLOTHES AND PROPS

Wear a baseball cap, jeans, and a shirt. Wear a large belt and carry an axe.

Make an Axe
You need:

- A long cardboard tube from a used roll of paper towels or aluminum foil
- Some thin cardboard (an empty cereal box will do)
- Tape measure
- Glue
- Paint
- Scissors

1. Cut a piece of cardboard as shown, with an axe-shape at either end and a thinner strip in the middle.

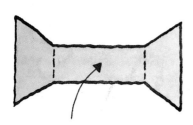

This strip should be long enough to fit around your tube. Measure it with a tape measure.

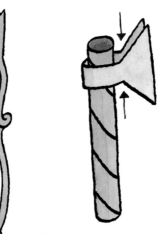

2. Glue the strip around the top of the tube and glue the axe heads together.

3. Once the glue is dry, paint your axe any color you like.

Face Painting Ideas for Mother
Make your cheeks rosy and wear some pretty lipstick.

Stage and Sounds

Once you have read the play through, you may want to perform it in front of an audience. If so, read through this section first. It has been kept very simple. You may want to add some extra performance ideas of your own during rehearsal.

COSTUME CHANGES

People who play more than one part will occasionally need to change their costumes. The stage directions tell you when to do this. Keep your costumes offstage and out of sight, perhaps behind a table covered with a tablecloth or on a table hidden behind an open door.

REHEARSING

Rehearse the play before you ask someone to watch.

PROPS

Position a chair on stage. You will need this to represent Grandma's bed. If you like, cover your legs with a blanket.

Keep any other props out of sight from the audience.

SOUNDS

Knocking on Grandma's door:
Knock on the back of your book or on a nearby chair.

Fighting:
Go offstage when the Wolf eats Grandma and later fights with the Woodcutter, so the audience can't see you. Then make shouting and scuffling noises as if you are fighting.

The Play

Storyteller

Once upon a time, there was a little girl named Red Riding Hood. She got her name because she wore a red cloak with a hood to keep herself warm in the winter.

The Storyteller points to Little Red Riding Hood and then to her Mother.

Storyteller

Red Riding Hood lived with her Mother on the edge of a thick forest. Her Grandmother lived on the other side of the forest at the end of a long winding path. One day Grandma became ill...

Mother

> Granny is not well today, Red Riding Hood. She won't feel like shopping, so I want you to take her a basket of food.

Mother packs a basket with goodies.

Red Riding
Hood

> Poor Granny. I'll do my best to cheer her up.

Red Riding Hood's mother hands her the basket of tasty food. As she waves goodbye, she gives her a warning...

Mother hands Red Riding Hood the basket. They wave to each other.

Mother

Stay on the path and don't talk to strangers, especially not wolves. Remember, never trust a Wolf!

Red Riding Hood sings softly as she carries the basket.

**Red Riding
Hood**

Tra la, la, la. What a lovely sunny day it is. What a pity poor Granny is too ill to get out of bed and enjoy the sunshine.

The Wolf pops up behind Red Riding Hood and whispers to himself.

Wolf

Ho, ho! Old Granny's stuck in bed, eh? I think I'll pay her a visit just in time for lunch.

The Wolf scampers off towards Grandma's cottage, chuckling softly to himself.

The Wolf chuckles. The noise makes Red Riding Hood jump.

Red Riding Hood

What was that? It must have been a bunny...

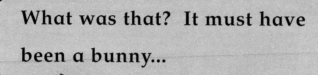

Storyteller

A bunny? Oh, dear me no. It wasn't a bunny. It was the wicked Wolf himself! Be careful Red Riding Hood!

14

Someone needs to do Grandma's voice here, though the audience doesn't need to see her. One of the other players could do it offstage.
Start by making a knocking noise (do it on the back of your book).

Grandma

Who is it?

Wolf
(pretending to be Red Riding Hood)

It's me,

Red Riding Hood.

Grandma

Oh, how lovely.

Come in, dear.

The door's open.

COSTUME CHANGE

The person playing the Wolf runs out of sight and pretends to have a fight, making shrieking and thumping noises. Then the Wolf comes back licking his lips, wearing the granny glasses, nightgown, and scarf over his ears (see page 7).

Wolf

Yum, yum! That Granny was delicious! My second course will be coming along in a minute.

If you wish, the Wolf can sit on a chair to represent Grandma's bed. His knees could be covered with a blanket. There is another knock on the door.

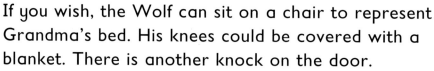

Red Riding Hood

Granny, it's Red Riding Hood.

Wolf (whispers to himself)

Oh, good. Here comes the rest of my lunch!

Wolf (pretending to be Grandma)

Come in, dear. The door's open.

Red Riding Hood

Hello, Granny. My, you look ill. I've brought you a basket of food to make you feel a little better.

Wolf
(pretending to be Grandma)

How kind. Come a little closer so I can see you...

Red Riding Hood puts her basket down and peers at the Wolf dressed as Grandma.

Red Riding Hood

Ooh, Granny. What big eyes you have!

Wolf
(pretending to be Grandma)

All the better to see you with, my dear!
Come a little closer.

Red Riding Hood

My, what big ears you have!

Wolf
(pretending
to be
Grandma)

All the better to hear you with, my dear!
Now come a little closer.

Red Riding Hood

Oh my, oh my. What big teeth you have!

Wolf

All the better to EAT you with, my dear!

The Wolf chases Red Riding Hood around.

Wolf

Come here, little girl!

I'm still hungry!

Red Riding Hood

Help, help!

Storyteller

Poor Red Riding Hood is about to become a Wolf snack. Then suddenly the door bursts open, and in strides the Woodcutter carrying his axe.

Woodcutter

What's all the noise?
Aha! So it's you,
you rotten Wolf!
I'll fix you,
my furry friend.

The Woodcutter chases the Wolf around with his axe.

Wolf

Help, help!

COSTUME CHANGE

The Wolf and the Woodcutter run out of sight, but you can still hear them shrieking and pretending to fight. While offstage, the person playing the Wolf takes off the wolf mask and gives it to the Woodcutter.

Woodcutter
(off-stage)

Chop, chop! We'll have no more trouble from you, Mr. Wolf! Now then ... let's see... Chop, chop. Aha, I thought so! Out you come, Granny!

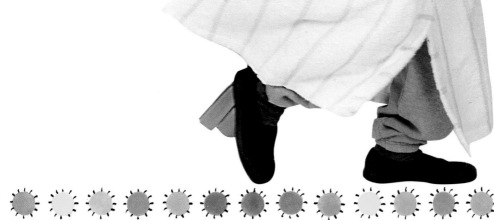

23

The Woodcutter appears carrying the wolf mask.

Oh thank you, Mr. Woodcutter!

Red
Riding
Hood

Red Riding
Hood hugs the
Woodcutter.

Woodcutter

The wicked Wolf is dead.

The Woodcutter
holds up the wolf
mask.

Storyteller

And so our story had a happy ending. Grandma was saved from the Wolf's tummy, Red Riding Hood got safely home, and the woods were never troubled by wolves again.

If you like, finish the play with a loud wolf howl!